The proper words in the proper places
are the true definition of style.

~ Jonathan Swift

STEVE FADIE

Words
to the
Rescue:

The sentiment guide for the tongue tied.

OrangeSky
B O O K S

This book is available at discount rates when purchased in bulk for premiums, sales promotions or fundraisers. Custom editions are also available. For information, contact the publisher: www.WordsToTheRescue.com

Library of Congress Control Number: 2007938381
ISBN: 978-0-98004-800-1

Cover and inside design: Ilya Hardey, David Barlow
Author photo: David Barlow

Printed in the United States of America

First printing, November 2007

Second printing, November 2008

Third printing, March 2011

Fourth printing, December 2011

Fifth printing, May 2012

Sixth printing, October 2012

Seventh printing, March 2013

Dedicated to everyone whose pencil
has ever been stuck in neutral.

A short saying often contains much wisdom.

~ Sophocles

Contents

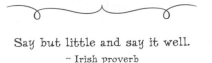

Say but little and say it well.
~ Irish proverb

Introduction

Have you ever wished you could express your feelings in writing, with just a few powerful words?

Like when you're giving flowers to a spouse or relative. And you want to write something clever on the enclosure card. Or when you're signing a birthday card at work. And three people have already scribbled "Best wishes." Or when you're sending a sympathy card. And you want to add a personal note.

These are times that call for one, two or three carefully chosen sentences. Or even just a few words. Words that bring a smile. Words that celebrate. Words that console. This book shows you how to write messages like that.

Flip through these pages and be inspired. Use the entries as is. Or personalize them. Where underlines appear, fill in your own words. Let your words flow naturally. From your heart.

Focus on how you feel about the person to whom you're writing. And the things that make them unique.

Toss bits and pieces of one message with parts of others. Don't limit yourself to the obvious section. Need a birthday message? Check the Thinking of You, Encouragement and Friendship sections.

From witty to sentimental to thoughtful you'll find a variety of styles. Because everyone has their own way of communicating. And since the most succinct messages are often the most powerful, every entry is 30 words or less.

Years ago, as I was ordering sympathy flowers, a florist asked the inevitable question. "What would you like the card to say?" I was at a loss. Totally stuck. I wrote this book so that you'll always have a quick source of inspiration.

In this age of fleeting e-mails, a handwritten note is the most personal gift you can give. I hope you will use this book, and your own natural eloquence, to create word gifts for the special people in your life.

~ Steve Fadie

1.
Anniversary

Words of love are works of love.
~ William R. Alger

Kisses, hugs and hoorahs on
your marriage milestone.

∽

It gets better every year.
Know what? So do you.

∽

Congratulations to <u>Wilma</u> and <u>Fred</u>,
who've been together since the stone age.

∽

You can't do any better in life
than to spend it with your best friend.

To personalize a message, insert your own words where you see <u>underlines</u>.

Our life is like a roller coaster. It's got ups and downs, screaming and a whole lot of fun.

∽

Loving you has been the most satisfying and rewarding part of my life.

∽

You'll never change. After all these years you're just as <u>beautiful</u> as <u>when we met</u>.

∽

<u>Eight</u> roses. <u>Eight</u> awesome years.

∽

The longer I know you, the more I <u>appreciate</u> you.

You don't have to be a poet to put your feelings in words. Just be real.

words to the rescue ⎰ Anniversary

Lucky, lucky me, to have <u>found a guy</u>
as <u>fantastic</u> as you.

⌒

How fortunate a traveler I am,
to share this journey with you.

⌒

<u>Partners</u> in laughter — and in tears.
It's good to celebrate <u>16</u> years.

⌒

Happy <u>23rd</u> to my forever source of <u>strength</u>.

⌒

I must have done something right
to deserve a <u>lady</u> like you.

For more Anniversary ideas, see Fast Phrases, page 132.

Anniversary kisses to
my partner in passion.

❧

We've worked so hard to get this far,
we deserve a tropical vacation.
(Or at least a <u>new dishwasher</u>.)

❧

How much stinkin' happiness
can one <u>guy</u> take?

❧

We don't need a lot to be happy.
Just each other.

❧

I've made some poor choices.
But choosing you to be my <u>wife</u>?
Smartest thing I ever did.

When you write from the heart you can't go wrong.

I hope the two of you are
smelling the roses, and savoring the
success of your <u>25-year</u> partnership.

∽

You deserve an award. Being married
for <u>40</u> years is a rarity <u>we're</u> thrilled
to celebrate with you.

∽

On your <u>20th</u> anniversary, it's a <u>pleasure</u>
<u>and a privilege</u> to wish our <u>good friends</u>
all the joy two hearts can hold.

∽

Love isn't perfect.
But when it embraces two people like you
for so many years, that's as close
to superb as it gets.

Mark their milestone with a note of gratitude.

Hey, if you guys hadn't found each other <u>20</u> years ago, I wouldn't be. Thanks. Your <u>son</u>.

◠◡◠

If I was writing "How To Be Married Forever," a picture of you two would be on the cover.

◠◡◠

To the couple who puts the "art" in partnership.

◠◡◠

Here's to love for the rest of <u>your</u> lives, and the best of <u>your</u> lives.

◠◡◠

Dear Mom and Dad: Thanks for being the glue that holds our family together.

For related messages, check the Romance & Fun section, page 95.

2.
Apology

Love me when I least deserve it.
That's when I really need it.
~ Swedish proverb

<u>Beth</u>: You are the most important person in the world. It's time I treat you that way.

OOOPS. I goofed big time. Can you see it in your heart to forgive me?

If I had a magic eraser, I would wipe away all the <u>dumb</u> things I <u>said last night</u>.

Elephants never forget. But I sure do. Sorry for <u>being so late</u>.

To personalize a message, insert your own words where <u>underlines</u> appear.

words to the rescue 〉 Apology

For what I did, I should be roped to a prickly cactus surrounded by poisonous snakes.

I hope these flowers get me in the door. 'Cause what I did, I won't do no more.

I've gone and put myself in the doghouse again. I beg your mercy.

I'll do just about anything to get back on your good side. Even take you shoe shopping.

It should come as no surprise that the Foot-in-Mouth Association has asked me to be their spokesperson.

When writing an apology note, be specific, genuine and sincere.

words to the rescue ⟩ **Apology**

Life is full of hard times.
This is one of them.
My hope is we can <u>work it out</u>.

༄

Guilty as charged, your honor.
How can I make it up to you?

༄

I understand why you are so <u>upset</u>.
I let you down and I'm sorry.

༄

Please forgive my <u>erratic behavior</u>.
It's not like me to <u>act that way</u>.

༄

I'm sorry I <u>disappointed you</u>. I've learned
<u>an important life lesson</u> because of it.

For more Apology ideas, see Fast Phrases, page 133.

) Apology

You have good reason to be <u>angry</u>.
Please know you are the last person
in the world I would want to hurt.

✑

There are over 6000 languages in the world.
But none has the words to say how sorry I am.

✑

Apologies from my heart, my soul
and, most of all, me.

✑

Everyone makes mistakes. It's just that
mine are BIGGER than most.

✑

I know these <u>flowers</u> can't make up for
<u>what I did</u>. But please know how deeply
sorry I am for <u>my mistake</u>.

Let your words flow from your true feelings of regret.

To hurt someone as <u>kind</u> as you is the
most <u>ridiculous</u> thing I've ever done.

I double love you.
That's why I would never intentionally
do a single thing to <u>hurt</u> you.

I should have known better. After all,
I know you and you are the best.

I apologize with every fiber of my being.

I've got this hug I've been wanting
to give you for a long time.

To create an original note, combine bits and pieces of messages you see here.

I must have been brain dead.
Because I was dead wrong.

∽

If I could take it back, I would do it in a
New York minute. I was <u>inconsiderate</u> and <u>rude</u>.

∽

Please accept <u>these flowers</u>
with an apology and a hope, that someday
you might forgive this dope.

∽

Sometimes people <u>do stupid stuff</u> for no
reason. I'm guilty. I apologize.

∽

I wouldn't blame you if you never
forgive me. But I'm <u>praying</u> that you will.

Check the Thinking of You section, page 125, for more inspiration.

3.
Birthday

A heart that loves is always young.
~ Greek proverb

Don't think of yourself as old.
Chronologically gifted sounds much cooler.

Age. It's all good.

There are advantages to getting old. Please let
<u>me</u> know when you find out what they are.

Best wishes to my <u>friend Jim</u> on the <u>20th</u>
anniversary of your <u>29th</u> birthday.

To personalize a message, insert your own words where <u>underlines</u> appear.

Have a King Tut day, oh ancient one.

❧

I refuse to make a joke about age.
(Laughing only causes wrinkles.)

❧

<u>45</u> isn't old...for a tree.

❧

To <u>Eddie</u> the computer guy:
Now downloading birthday wishes.
Approximate time: <u>645 minutes</u>.

❧

At an age when most people are sitting in
rocking chairs, you're sitting on top of the
world. Keep your youthful spirit glowing.

A birthday gift doesn't have to come in a box. Give them a note filled with love.

The earth is 4.5 billion years old.
Relatively speaking, this makes you
<u>a spring chicken</u>.

❧

There's no such thing as a midlife crisis.
It's more like a total meltdown.

❧

Here's to the oldie but goodie.

❧

H-B to you from me.

❧

<u>Forty</u> is a <u>fantastic</u> age to be.
Too bad <u>we</u> passed it
a long time ago.

Give them something they'll keep: a personal note from you.

Remember, if you've got your hair, nothing else matters. Hope you're aging well.

∽

Old and pudgy? No way.
You're more bold and edgy.

∽

We may be over the hill.
But we're not over the thrill.

∽

To my <u>handsome handyman</u>, who never met a <u>power tool</u> he didn't like.

∽

Three things happen as you grow older.
First, your memory goes.
I forget the other two.

For more ideas, check the Congratulations section, page 39.

Don't worry. Age is just a number.
(In our case, a big number.)

✑

Birthdays are good for us.
The more we have, the longer we live.
~ Author unknown

✑

As long as we keep laughing at our own
jokes, that's all that matters.

✑

To <u>my</u> down-to-earth <u>buddy</u> who's
older than <u>dirt</u>.

✑

Some <u>people</u> always look the same
no matter how old they get. Unfortunately,
you and I are not among them.

The Thinking of You section, page 125, may also inspire you.

Happy birthday to the <u>beautiful aunt</u> who not
only takes the cake, <u>she</u> makes it too.

⟨∽⟩

<u>Grandpa</u>, you are <u>wonderful, unique</u>
and loved, today and everyday.

⟨∽⟩

To my stylish <u>niece</u> who's forever cool.

⟨∽⟩

If love is a journey, there's nobody else
I'd rather travel with. Happy <u>26th</u>.

⟨∽⟩

I am a better <u>wife, mother and
human being</u> because of you.

For more Birthday ideas see Fast Phrases, page 134.

Time flies, days pass and years go by. But you'll always be the same <u>sweet sister</u> to me.

∽⌒

Did I ever tell you how totally glad I am that you and I share the same genes?

∽⌒

God's richest blessings to <u>our soulful cousin</u>.

∽⌒

Dear <u>Uncle Mike</u>: you're <u>80?</u> That's totally crazy. Love from <u>your fan club</u>.

∽⌒

Your birthday: a time to reflect on blessings. Like having a <u>terrific brother</u> like me.

Celebrate life's happy times with a handwritten note.

Birthday

Have the best birthday day ever, <u>giggles</u>.
You make me laugh so hard I can
water plants with my tears.

⌀

I don't tell you this enough, <u>Nicholas</u>, but you
are totally loved, today and every day.

⌀

They don't make kids like they used to.
They make them better, and you're proof.

⌀

What did one light bulb say to the
other? I wuv you watts and watts.

⌀

Happy birthday to a little girl who's so sweet,
she puts sugar out of a job.

Think of 5 admirable traits of the birthday person. List them in a note.

Birthday

To a <u>terrific nephew</u> on <u>his</u> birthday.
You're smart, funny and kind.
(You take after <u>me</u>.)

❧

I hope someday, <u>Jose</u>, you have a son as <u>cool</u>
as the one <u>your mother and I</u> have.

❧

Keep hitting them out of the park, slugger.
Or should I say, super boy.

❧

Whoopie-do-da-day. <u>Angie</u> is <u>seven</u>.
Girl power forever.

❧

Buy something <u>totally ridiculous</u>
with this money. Remember:
You can never have too much <u>fun</u>.

E-mail is great. But nothing can replace the warmth of your handwritten note.

⸙ Birthday

When you were born, I knew you would
grow up to be a <u>handsome, intelligent
young man</u>. Looks like <u>grandma</u>'s right again.

⌒⌒

It's your day to go crazy and wild. Hey, isn't
that what you do every day?

⌒⌒

Happy birthday to the most <u>fantabulous
little girl</u> this side of a <u>rainbow</u>.

⌒⌒

<u>Alex</u>, you're no angel. Just the closest
thing to it a <u>grandma</u> could ever want.

⌒⌒

One two three. Do re mi. You're
the best <u>niece</u> I ever did see.

Say more than just Happy Birthday. Tell them what they mean to you.

Birthday

Yo <u>Colton</u>. Rock on birthday bud.

❧

Happy <u>9th</u> birthday to the <u>girl</u> who will always be the brightest star in <u>my</u> sky.

❧

X-tra love to <u>Jason</u> on your birthday. You're x-tra cool, x-tra smart and x-tra fun.

❧

You stole <u>my</u> heart when you were born. <u>Ten</u> years later, you've still got it.

❧

Lots of laughs and lots of love too. <u>We're</u> proud of you <u>son</u>, H-B-2-U.

The Thinking of You section, page 125, may spark other ideas.

My wish for you Ming: A day and a year
as adventurous as you are.

⌒⟋⌒

No matter how many candles on the cake,
you're still the one that lights up the room.

⌒⟋⌒

Please thank your mother for me. Anyone who
can bring a person like you into the world
deserves a standing ovation.

⌒⟋⌒

Congrats to the guy who's always
the life of the party. Hey, without you,
there'd be no party.

⌒⟋⌒

To my 29-and-holding birthday bud.

A birthday is the perfect time to say, "I'm glad you're in my life."

Forty is the old age of youth.
Fifty is the youth of old age.
~ French proverb

∽◌

To an <u>office mate</u> who has a
<u>remarkable way</u> of making others feel <u>good</u>.

∽◌

We turn not older with years,
but newer every day.
~ Emily Dickinson

∽◌

All the best, to the best.

∽◌

Hugs to <u>an enlightened friend</u> who never
lets me forget how <u>brilliant</u> life can be.

For more ideas, check the Friendship section, page 73.

From the time you were <u>a wee little one</u>,
you were destined for life in the Fab Lane.

⌒⌒

May the coming year dump a truckload of
<u>blessings</u> and a ton of <u>laughs</u> on you.

⌒⌒

Youth is a gift of nature.
Age is <u>a work of art.</u>
~ Author unknown

⌒⌒

May your days be good
and long upon the earth.
~ Apache blessing

⌒⌒

The older the <u>violin</u>,
the <u>sweeter the music</u>.

Spouse's birthday? Check the Romance & Fun section, page 95.

From one <u>cheeseball</u> to another:
Have <u>an excellent</u> birthday.

❧

To me, old age is always ten
years older than I am.
~ John Burroughs

❧

Luv -n- you all ways.

❧

Now that you're <u>50</u>, you know all those
things you thought were so important?
They're not.

❧

Grow old with me, the best is yet to be.
~ Robert Browning

Give what nobody else can. A handmade card in your own writing.

Birthday

Life: The adventure continues.

∽

You're huggable. Lovable.
Simply irresistible. Enjoy.

∽

Hugs and kisses to the best CEO
(Chief Entertainment Officer)
a <u>family</u> could have.

∽

No rhymes. No sappy words.
Just a note on your birthday to tell you
how <u>fantastic</u> you are.

∽

Youth is a wonderful thing.
What a crime to waste it on children.
~ George Bernard Shaw

For more Birthday ideas, see Fast Phrases, page 134.

4.
Congratulations

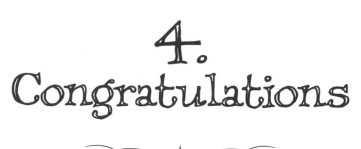

Who is the happiest?
He who values the merits of others.
~ Goethe

Who said the sky's the limit?
You've just proven otherwise.

Hey bigshot. Way to go.

I can't think of anyone who deserves the
<u>warm glow of success</u> more than you.

Congrats: Your new job sounds perfect.
Rats: We can't gab by the coffeepot anymore.

To personalize a message, insert your own words where <u>underlines</u> appear.

Congratulations

ACHIEVEMENT

To a <u>talented woman</u> who's come a long way.
And is going a lot further.

∽

You deserve a big hand. And a big hug.

∽

Kudos kiddo.

∽

A standing ovation to the incredible shrinking
<u>man</u>. Bravo on the slim new you.

∽

To the brightest star on the stage tonight.
You glow girl. <u>Your mother and I</u>
are mega-proud.

Your positive words in a note can provide affirmation and motivation to others.

Congratulations

ACHIEVEMENT

Consider me an official member of the
"Jason Rules" fan club.

∽

Eeeee-gads you're good.

∽

The people who move ahead in life exude
talent, wit and enthusiasm. Just like you.

∽

Congratulations to the lady
who could sell tuxes to penguins.

∽

Your promotion proves one thing all dairy
farmers know. The cream rises to the top.

Need more ideas? See Fast Phrases, page 135.

BABY

Having a baby will open your heart
more than you ever imagined.

∽

If I were a little one getting ready to be born,
I would order up parents just like
you and <u>Don</u>.

∽

Another heart to love.
Another tax deduction to take.

∽

You are embarking on an amazing journey.
The ride can be bumpy, so buckle up...and enjoy.

∽

It's a pleasure and a thrill for us to extend
our best wishes to you and <u>Jeanna</u> as you
prepare <u>for your first child</u>.

To personalize a message, insert your own words where <u>underlines</u> appear.

Congratulations

BABY

Baby blessings.
Gigantic congratulations.

⚯

Everything you hear about being
a parent is true. It's the most <u>amazing</u>
experience of your life.

⚯

Congratulations on the growing <u>Paxton</u>
<u>dynasty</u>. You'll be a <u>fantastic mother</u>.

⚯

Take it from someone who's been there.
They grow up fast. Savor every crazy minute.

⚯

I can't think of two more <u>caring</u> parents
than both of you.

A birth changes a family forever. Honor the parents with a personal note.

BABY

A new baby. What more could you ask for?
Other than sleep, that is.

∽

To hug and to hold, from this day on.

∽

To my <u>little brother Joel</u> and
<u>sister-in-law</u> <u>Laura</u>. You've done
the family proud once again.

∽

Twinkle twinkle little star,
what an <u>attractive</u> family you are.

∽

What's one more diaper to change?
You're already pros at it.

Celebrate the happy times in life. Write a personal note.

Congratulations

BABY

The tree of life has just grown another branch.
Congratulations to the old roots.

❧

Accolades to the MVPs.
(Most Valuable Parents.)

❧

With joy, reverence and awe, we stretch out
our arms in welcome of your new <u>son Alex</u>.

❧

May love, health and wisdom
embrace your <u>new daughter Maya</u>.
May countless blessings be <u>hers</u>.

❧

Congratulations on your new sunrise.

For more inspiration, see Fast Phrases, page 135.

BABY

We hear <u>the new kid on the block</u> is amazing.
Must be <u>he</u> takes after mom and dad.

∽

Every good gift and every
perfect gift is from above.
~ The Bible

∽

Miracles DO happen. This one couldn't
have graced a <u>more deserving couple</u>.

∽

Corks are popping. Flags are flying. Angels are
rejoicing. Thumbs up to the <u>Cortez</u> clan.

∽

May joy continue to shine on the <u>Alexanders</u>,
as it has with the birth of <u>Carter</u>.

Did you know? Some people hold on to cards and notes for a lifetime.

BABY

Tickled pink about your new arrival.

❧

Coochie coochie coo.
Parenthood is good for you.

❧

Sharing your joy.

❧

It takes <u>character, strength</u> and a
<u>good moral compass</u> to be successful parents,
all of which the two of you have in droves.

❧

Being a <u>mom</u> is no easy task.
Seeing the way you've lived your life,
I have no doubt you'll be a <u>stellar</u> one.

The Thinking of You section, page 125, may also spark ideas.

GRADUATION

Hey computer whiz: Go kick giga-butt.

∽

Life is a garden. Get out there and dig it.

∽

Always bear in mind that your own
resolution to success is more
important than any other thing.
~ Abraham Lincoln

∽

Live a good and honorable life.
Then when you get older and think back,
you'll be able to enjoy it a second time.
~ The 14th Dalai Lama

∽

Be creative. Be curious. Most of all, keep
being the wonderful young lady you are.

To personalize a message, insert your own words where underlines appear.

GRADUATION

Wherever you go, go with all your heart.
~ Confucius

❦

You've come a long way, <u>Jamile</u>, and proven yourself to be a <u>strong, capable young man</u>.

❦

Follow the cut of your jib, the ilk of your own nature. Be yourself and you'll <u>go far</u>.

❦

Celebrate life. Learn a lot. Embrace love. And eat lots of fish. It's good for your brain.

❦

As your <u>aunt</u>, I wish I was there to give you a pinch on the cheek. But since I can't be, let me say "Wooohooo <u>Jeffery</u>, you did it!"

Graduation is a rite of passage. Your words can help commemorate the occasion.

words to the rescue ⟩ # Congratulations

GRADUATION

Nobody's ever been more
proud of you than <u>we are</u> today.

◦◦

Ya done good, kid.

◦◦

Getting your <u>degree</u> took dedication,
hard work and tons of get-up-and-go.
I'm exhausted just thinking about it.

◦◦

Eight words for success:
Do what you love. Love what you do.

◦◦

As you enter the next phase of your life,
<u>Chris</u>, remember: <u>Believe in yourself.</u>
<u>Never give up</u>. And don't forget to <u>floss</u>.

Share your knowledge and experience in a personal note.

GRADUATION

<u>Son</u>, your future is like <u>our</u> love for you,
Unlimited.

∽

Good going <u>Marika</u>. You've climbed so many
mountains, <u>we</u> can't wait to see what's next.

∽

Hot dang. You did it.
Just like <u>we</u> knew you could.

∽

Don't be like the cat who wanted a fish
but was afraid to get his paws wet.
~ Shakespeare

∽

Be amazing. Be bold. Be a hero.
Be wise. Be healthy. Be grateful. Be you.

The best greeting cards are the ones you write yourself.

words to the rescue ⎰ Congratulations

NEW BUSINESS

There's no business
like your own business.

∽

Don't forget a sweater.
It's windy on the mountaintop.

∽

Tell your new boss I'm rooting for <u>her</u>.

∽

Advice for the new business owner:
Keep your head up. Expenses down.
And the coffee on.

∽

If anyone can make this venture
work, it's you, <u>Ivan</u>. You've got that
magical thing called "it."

Don't just say congratulations. Say how happy you are with their success.

NEW BUSINESS

Congratulations on <u>going out on your own</u>.
With your <u>talent</u>, I know you'll <u>succeed</u>.

∽

It takes G.U.T.S. to start a business.
Gumption. Uncommon initiative.
Talent. And Smarts.

∽

I saw the angel in the marble
and carved until I set him free.
~ Michelangelo

∽

May you prosper in your new location, with
more customers than the stars in the sky.

∽

Best wishes to the new CEO:
Chief Everything Officer.

Everybody needs encouragement. Your personal note is like a pat on the back.

NEW HOME

Everyone needs a peaceful retreat
from <u>the chaos of the world.</u>
Kudos on finding yours.

༄

Home is where the art is.
[Give with framed print.]

༄

Welcome to the neighborhood.
We're glad you're here.

༄

Advice for new <u>homeowners</u>:
Get a roll of duct tape for every room.
It's the quicker-fixer-upper.

༄

The new castle is <u>awesome</u>.

Use your note to complement their good taste.

NEW HOME

Like grandma's handmade quilt, may your new home keep you oh so cozy. Enjoy.

～⌒

Blessings to the <u>Mayvilles</u> as you live, laugh, love and put down roots in your new home. [Give with a tree.]

～⌒

Kick back and relax. You'll be making regular runs to the hardware store soon enough.

～⌒

Now that you've filled your home with furniture, you can start filling it with memories. [Give with a photo album.]

～⌒

Welcome to the Mortgage Club.

Buying a new house is a big event. Applaud them with your message.

NEW HOME

New marriage. New mortgage.
Wonder what's next?
You know. Now get busy.

❧

Congrats on your new R&R headquarters.
We're dubbing it the new <u>party central</u>.

❧

Wall-to-wall happiness in your new <u>abode</u>.

❧

Grass, garage, garden and your own <u>washing
machine</u>. Do miracles never cease?

❧

A big old couch and a fireplace,
with friends and family all around.
That's livin' the dream.

See Fast Phrases, page 135 for more Congratulations messages.

words to the rescue ⟩ Congratulations

RETIREMENT

If you ever miss the <u>corporate jungle</u>, feel free
to swing by and we'll trade places for <u>a week</u>.

✑

The stars have aligned in your favor.
May this new phase of your life open
a universe of possibilities.

✑

Congratulations on a <u>long, successful</u> career.
Good luck <u>at the fishing hole</u>.

✑

If success is gained by those who
<u>work hard</u>, <u>laugh often</u> and <u>love a lot</u>,
you are a triple winner.

✑

May you look back on the past with as much
pleasure as you look forward to the future.
~ Irish verse

For more ideas, check out the Friendship section, page 73.

RETIREMENT

Now that you're retired, <u>Gary</u>, you'll have
lots of time on your hands. Spend it wisely.
Get into as much trouble as you can.

❧

I'm so jealous. You get to be
<u>off globetrotting</u>, while I'm stuck
here <u>sharpening pencils</u>.

❧

Always remember to squeeze the day.
Life is juicier that way.

❧

Congratulations from
the bottom of my <u>briefcase</u>.

❧

It's not an ending.
It's a totally new beginning.

See Fast Phrases, page 135, for more congratulatory words.

RETIREMENT

At a time when I should be giving you a gift,
I realize it's YOU who's given me a gift.
Thanks for showing me the value of hard work.

∾

Retirement? What retirement?
If I know you <u>Linda</u>, your schedule is
booked for the next <u>two decades</u>.

∾

Just because you're retiring doesn't mean
your dreams are. Prepare for take-off.

∾

You deserve to shine. I mean, what
else is a star supposed to do?

∾

Old golfers never stop hitting the green,
<u>we</u> just keep putting along.

If there's any event that deserves applause, it's the end of a long career.

words to the rescue ∫ Congratulations

WEDDING

Nothing makes this <u>old couple</u> happier than
to see two people so perfectly matched.
Especially when they are as <u>nice</u> as both of you.

✎

First rule for a successful marriage:
Relinquish control to wife.

✎

Some say love is all you need.
From my experience, <u>taking turns
doing the dishes</u> can't hurt either.

✎

<u>Hugs and prayers</u> for two
<u>talented young people</u> embarking on
the journey of a lifetime.

✎

Blessings, bravos, congrats, kudos and kisses.

The best greeting card is the one you write yourself.

WEDDING

Everything that's happened has brought you to this <u>spectacular</u> moment. <u>Our love</u> is with you.

∽

After the excitement of your <u>gigantic rockin'</u> wedding has passed, you'll have something that lasts forever. Bills.

∽

Best of luck you two.
Although with your obvious <u>affection</u> for each other, <u>I</u> doubt you'll need it.

∽

The <u>adorable</u> baby <u>we</u> met <u>on her first day home from the hospital,</u> has blossomed into a <u>beautiful bride.</u>

∽

Soul-felt wishes for a <u>happy and abundant life together.</u>

Share your lighthearted marriage advice in a note. They'll love it.

words to the rescue ⎰ # Congratulations

WEDDING

As you enter the sacred union of marriage,
may the promise you make today guide
you in good times, bad times and
every-day-of-your-life times.

≈

Marriage is not easy. But it's obvious to <u>me</u>
you two have what it takes to make it work.

≈

<u>Cindy</u> + <u>Joe</u> = happiness and humor =
long life together.

≈

May the <u>joy</u> you share today be
just a taste of what's to come.

≈

A new adventure. A sunrise. A path untaken.
A warm wish to an <u>exceptional couple</u>.

See Fast Phrases, page 135 for more Congratulations ideas.

5.
Encouragement

The best way to cheer yourself up
is to try to cheer somebody else up.
~ Mark Twain

U-R so GR-8.

As the drain said to the sink,
I'm always at your disposal.

Drum roll please...I declare this official
Appreciate <u>Debbie</u> Day. Watch for
a surprise when I get home.

We'll make it through this together.
You hold me. I'll hold you.

To personalize a message, insert your own words where <u>underlines</u> appear.

words to the rescue } # Encouragement

<u>We</u> believe in you.
<u>We</u> support you.
<u>We</u> applaud you.

∽

If you need <u>me</u>, just say "YO."

∽

Win, lose or draw, <u>we'll</u> always be
your <u>number one fans</u>.

∽

Your <u>family</u> is behind you. Always.
And all ways.

∽

You've done so much for us <u>Dad</u>,
<u>we'd</u> like to try and return the favor.

Help others stay motivated to achieve their goals. Encourage them with a note.

Encouragement

May you have warm words on a cold day,
a full moon on a dark night, and a smooth
road all the way to your door.
~ Irish toast

❧

You were on a magic carpet ride and the rug
was pulled out from under you. I want to help.

❧

No reason. No season.
Just a <u>wink</u> from me to you.

❧

Let's get the <u>music</u> back in your life.

❧

In the spirit of someone that wants to see
you succeed, let me say this. <u>Dump the jerk</u>.

For more encouraging words, see Fast Phrases, page 136.

Encouragement

A rough <u>year</u> past. A better one coming.

☙

I'm so sorry about <u>what happened at work</u>.
Stay strong, <u>Carol</u>. I'll bring over some
<u>tacos</u> for <u>the family</u> on <u>Saturday</u>.

☙

Through all the storms,
you've kept smiling. I have no doubt
your <u>faith</u> will see you through again.

☙

Time for a little soul cradling.

☙

My wish for you is
100% pure <u>outrageous joy</u>.

Everyone needs encouragement. With just paper and a stamp, you can supply it.

Encouragement

Every diva deserves her day.
But, girl, you deserve a whole year.

༺∽༻

Keep on keepin' on.

༺∽༻

To my favorite golfer on <u>tournament day</u>.
May the course be with you.

༺∽༻

Remember it takes both rain
and sun to make a rainbow.

༺∽༻

Things have got to get better.
With all <u>we've</u> been through,
the only way to go is UP.

A handwritten note is one of the most personal gifts you can give.

Not until we are lost
do we begin to find ourselves.
~ Henry David Thoreau

∽

Life is full of rainstorms.
I'm your big umbrella.

∽

He who has help has hope,
and he who has hope has everything.
~ Arabic proverb

∽

You've suffered a setback.
It's frustrating. Keep your eyes on the goal
and your thoughts focused.

∽

Nothing shall be impossible unto you.
~ The Bible

For more ideas, check the Thinking of You section, page 125.

Encouragement

I'm here when you need me.
And even when you don't

≈

Even a small star shines in the darkness.
~ Finnish proverb

≈

I have not failed. I've just found
10,000 ways that won't work.
~ Thomas Edison

≈

Open your mind, heart and soul.
You'll find the answer.

≈

Anyone who has never made a mistake
has never tried anything new.
~ Albert Einstein

Why wait for a special occasion? Send your encouraging words today.

Encouragement

You're going to be fine. Just remember this:
Time wounds all heels.

⌇

When <u>a heart has been broken</u>, I always
offer this advice: <u>Eat chocolate</u>.

⌇

You know that tune from TV,
"You're gonna make it after all?"
That's your new theme song.

⌇

Stop me if I'm wrong. But last time I looked,
you were a <u>strong, intelligent person</u>
capable of <u>making a great life for yourself</u>.

⌇

You can lean on me for
whatever, whenever, forever.

The Fast Phrases Friendship section, page 137, may also be of help.

Encouragement

Congratulations for having
the courage <u>to make a change</u>.

∽

Trust your heart.
It will show you the way.

∽

If you need a shoulder, mine's available 24/7.
(Tissues included.)

∽

I care very much about how you feel.

∽

Change is <u>a rocky road</u>.
Just take one step. Then another.
And keep on doing it.

You can't go wrong when you write from your heart.

Encouragement

I believe with all my heart that <u>good things</u>
are <u>on the horizon</u> for you.

❧

Faith can move mountains.
But first you've got to move your butt.

❧

I know you well. And I know the strength
is in you to weather this storm.

❧

Stay strong. Keep your heart open.

❧

Hope it helps a little for you to know
you're not just in my thoughts,
you're 100% of them.

See Fast Phrases, page 136, for more encouraging words.

6.
Friendship

The only way to have a friend is to be one.
~ Ralph Waldo Emerson

We've known each other since the stone ages.
Me caveman. You <u>friend</u>.

I'm rich. I have the good fortune
of having you as a <u>chum</u>.

True blue. That describes you.

There you go again. Performing your
<u>magic feats</u> of friendship.

To personalize a message, insert your own words where <u>underlines</u> appear.

Friends like you make <u>this world</u>
a <u>better</u> place for me.

༄

For your kind nature, I am <u>forever grateful</u>.
(Your <u>punny jokes</u> are another story.)

༄

A bud for my bud.
[Give with a rose or beer.]

༄

We don't have much time on earth.
What we do have is <u>friends</u> to make
our time more enjoyable.

༄

Our brain waves must be set to the same
frequency. How else would you account for
knowing <u>what I'm feeling</u> before even I do.

Did you know? Some people save cards and notes for a lifetime.

Friendship

It's good to know you've got my back.
(I've got the front pretty much covered.)

∽

I'm thankful to have you as a friend
who's kind to me even when I'm miserable.

∽

You overwhelm me with awesomeness.

∽

Good friends are rare. But you?
An endangered species.

∽

You're Lucy to my Ethel,
Johnny to my Ed.
I wouldn't have it any other way.

See Fast Phrases, page 137, for more Friendship ideas.

When you've found a <u>friend</u> who's
<u>the real thing</u>, you've found a keeper.

∽

A tisket. A tasket.
You're wonderfully fantastic.

∽

When it comes to the art of <u>friendship</u>,
<u>Picasso's</u> got nothing on you.

∽

Thanks for understanding me.
Even when I don't understand myself.

∽

In the garden of life,
your thumb isn't just green,
it's brown from helping me out of the mud.

The Thinking of You section, page 125, may also be helpful.

Friendship

Even when I'm acting like a <u>goofball</u>,
you don't care. It's nice to have a <u>friend</u>
who doesn't care.

❧

You've shown me that <u>friendship</u> isn't a big
thing. It's a million little things.

❧

Everyone needs a <u>sidekick</u>. Who else is gonna
kick you in the side now and then?

❧

No road is long with good company.
~ Turkish proverb

❧

You're not just one-of-a-kind.
You're my favorite kind.

Why wait for a special occasion to tell a friend you care?

words to the rescue } Friendship

A faithful friend is the medicine of life.
~ Apocrypha

૭⌒૭

Sometimes I just can't see the way.
Thanks for looking out for me.

૭⌒૭

You're great. Who else can I tell I got a great
deal on <u>toilet paper</u> and have them
be happy for me?

૭⌒૭

The <u>Good Guy</u> award goes to <u>Eric</u>, for
lifetime achievement in the art of <u>buddyship</u>.

૭⌒૭

What can I say?
We've been through it all together.

See Fast Phrases, page 137, for more Friendship ideas.

7.
Get Well

One kind word can warm three winter months.
~ Japanese proverb

Get well. Get better. Get back in bed.

Sending you <u>healing wishes</u>
nestled in <u>positive thoughts</u>.

Nobody wants to see you
back at 100% more than <u>I do</u>.

Chicken soup wishes <u>my friend</u>.

To personalize a message, insert your own words where <u>underlines</u> appear.

Get Well

May the sun smile on your days.
May the moon watch over your nights.

⌒

I wish I could weave a rainbow
into a blanket, wrap it around you,
and clear away every storm.

⌒

Please know you are <u>deeply loved</u>
by so many, including <u>me</u>.

⌒

I hope this note and the fact that you are
thought of <u>so fondly</u>, lift your spirits.

⌒

Thinking of you with <u>love and concern</u>.

Today, scribble a few lines to someone who would like to hear from you.

Get Well

Everybody wants time off.
But you didn't have to go and
<u>break a leg</u> to get it, did you?

❧

Why did the banana go to the doctor?
It wasn't peeling well.

❧

Get better and get back to work on the
double. <u>We</u> need you to bring <u>us donuts</u>.

❧

When you return, I expect a full report
on the joys of <u>hospital food</u>.

❧

Can't wait 'til you're out of those fuzzy
slippers and back on your feet.

For more Get Well ideas, see Fast Phrases, page 138.

Some folks will do anything to get flowers.
Be better soon.

∽◌∽

My greatest wish in this world?
For you to feel like yourself again.

∽◌∽

Your personal fan club is anxiously
awaiting your return.

∽◌∽

A get well wish to a <u>teacher</u> who cares,
from your <u>students</u> who do, too.

∽◌∽

Take good care of yourself.
You're too good <u>a person</u> to be so sick.

It takes five minutes to write them a note. But it can improve their day 500%.

Hope you're feeling a lot healthier, a lot happier, and a lot more like you, ASAP.

∽

I add my positive thoughts to yours to help you heal.

∽

Wish I could be there to fluff your pillow, cook you <u>chicken soup</u> and serve you <u>bon bons</u> in bed.

∽

Hang in there. Keep your spirit. Remain hopeful. Feel good.

∽

Maximum-strength get well wishes to <u>an aunt we</u> love to the max.

Write notes on ten postcards. Mail one a week to someone who needs cheer.

With love and prayers
from an <u>uncle</u> who cares.

∽

May the wind be at your back
and God at your side with every
tissue and aspirin you reach for.

∽

You have my prayerful and unending support.

∽

If God has an extra miracle,
I pray it be given to you.

∽

Thinking of you fondly...praying for
<u>your quick and total recovery.</u>

A handwritten note is one of the most personal gifts you can give.

{ **Get Well**

From far away, I'm thinking of you today.

∽

May the gift of good health
wrap you in its arms and soothe
your mind, body and soul.

∽

Where did the boat go when it wasn't
feeling well? Back to the doc.

∽

Take good care of yourself.
Your body needs you. <u>We</u> need you.

∽

Heal well. Heal soon.

Check the Thinking of You section, page 125, for more inspiration.

words to the rescue } **Get Well**

Can you hear the party horns?
Everyone is celebrating <u>your good news</u>.

⤫

I hope this <u>rough</u> time
in your life is soon behind you.

⤫

Hang in there, super trooper.

⤫

Rest, rest, rest, so you'll be
good, better, best.

⤫

Good wishes for good days.
Good riddance to doctor's visits.

Don't have a greeting card? A simple sheet of paper can make a fine note.

86

Blue skies. A carefree heart.
And gentle waves lapping on the beach.
That's my wish for you.

☙

T-L-C to you, from me.

☙

Without you here, it's like <u>a chocolate chip
cookie without the chips</u>. Hurry back.

☙

All <u>I</u> want is to see you <u>smile</u> again.

☙

Think of this note as a hug
tucked in an envelope.

E-mail is efficient. But nothing can replace the warmth of a handwritten note.

Get Well

Best of days to you.

∽

Drink hot tea. Eat toast.
Pull the covers over your head.

∽

Hurry up and get over this thing.
I miss the better you.

∽

God cares about you. So do I.

∽

Get well, but not too quick.
Enjoy every possible minute away
from this <u>nuthouse</u>.

See Fast Phrases, page 138, for more Get Well ideas.

8.
Goodbye & Miss You

Nothing makes the world seem so spacious
as to have friends at a distance.
~ Henry David Thoreau

Goodbye. Good luck. Good for you.

We'll miss your smile.
(We'll miss ours too.)

Adios amigos. Happy trails.

Make memories every day.
Life is too short not to.

To personalize a message, insert your own words where <u>underlines</u> appear.

Goodbye & Miss You

See you on the flip flop.

❧

Peace and soul grease.

❧

On your way to <u>the top</u>,
remember <u>us little people</u>.

❧

Sad you're leaving.
(Weep weep)
Glad for <u>your new opportunity</u>.
(Rah Rah)

❧

Whatever roads you take,
take time for detours.

A note about the good times you shared makes a thoughtful going-away gift.

{ # Goodbye & Miss You

Going nuts without you.
Come back before <u>I</u> crack up.

∽◦

I miss you so much,
even my <u>eyebrows</u> hurt.

∽◦

<u>I'm</u> having a hard time smiling,
without <u>my</u> daily fix of you.

∽◦

Can't W8-2-C-U.

∽◦

Everything seems dark
and grey without you here.

You can't go wrong when you write from your heart.

Goodbye & Miss You

In all my time away, one thing
has become clear. I need a bigger suitcase.
(Oh yeah, and I miss you.)

∽

Going bananas without you.
[Give banana bread.]

∽

I could never miss anyone or anything more
than I miss you. (Not counting football.)

∽

A day without you is like
a month without chocolate.

∽

I want nothing more than to snuggle up
and laugh our heads off like we used to.

Be genuine. Let your words flow from your true feelings.

Goodbye & Miss You

Roses are red. Without you, I'm blue.

I'm counting the days
'til I'm back with you and the kids.
Never dreamed I'd miss diaper duty.

So far away, so close in my thoughts.

I guess a man never really knows
how it feels to hurt inside, until
the woman he loves goes away.

Until the day I can hold you,
I'll be holding you front
and center in my thoughts.

Start your note with "Roses are red." Use your creativity. Take it from there.

Goodbye & Miss You

Every time I mark
a big red X on the calendar,
I count the days until you're back.

∽

Good thing I'm bald. Otherwise I'd be
tearing my hair out missing you.

∽

Let me leave you
with one of my favorite quotes:
"If you wake up, it's a good day."

∽

Missing you completely...desperately.

∽

It's been an honor working with you
and a real joy knowing you.

For more Goodbye & Miss You ideas, see Fast Phrases, page 139.

9.
Romance & Fun

Fill your paper with the breathings of your heart.
~ William Wordsworth

You're asking for trouble.
Where do I sign up?

Way too hot for words.

So easy to know.
So hard to forget.

To my <u>leading man</u>:
Let's get <u>an everything pizza</u>
and watch a movie tonight.

To personalize a message, insert your own words where <u>underlines</u> appear.

On a scale of <u>fabulous</u> to <u>stupendous</u>,
you get a double <u>marvelous</u>.

∽

If you look up "<u>beautiful</u>" in the dictionary,
guess whose name is there?
That's right. Mine.

∽

I <u>like</u> you.
You're almost as <u>bizarre</u> as I am.

∽

To the <u>guy</u> who makes me <u>smile</u>
for no reason at all.

∽

Would it be presumptuous to call you
absolutely scrumptious?

You don't have to be a poet to put your feelings in writing. Just be real.

You're so dang sweet...
I get cavities just thinking about you.

You're so dang sweet...
I get cavities just thinking about you.

∽

If our lives were a movie, what would you
like the next scene to be?

∽

Roses are red. Some are white.
Let's celebrate <u>us</u> tonight.
[Give with roses.]

∽

Tonight's forecast: Flurries of <u>passion</u>.

∽

Please join me for a little <u>food</u>.
A little <u>wine</u>.
And lots of <u>time together</u>.

For more Romance & Fun ideas, see Fast Phrases, page 140.

Romance & Fun

Your <u>love</u> never stops amazing me.
And crazing me.

Grateful that you and me are we.

I'm not just mad about you.
I'm abnormally insane.

Coming home is a lot more fun
with you here.

Let's see, how can I say this?
<u>Brenda</u>, I love you even more than my <u>car</u>.

For more inspiration, see the Thinking of You section, page 125.

Romance & Fun

To the kindred soul who
taught me how to love.

～

My <u>affection</u> for you? Two words:
<u>Endless. Everlasting.</u>

～

For your smiles in the morning and
your warm goodnight hugs.

～

Love isn't some abstract concept reserved
for Valentine's Day cards. It's what you and
I quietly share every day.

～

My philosophy of life is simple:
Making you happy, makes me happy.

When you write from your heart, you can't go wrong.

"Nunc scio quit sit amor."
Latin: Now I know what love is.
~ Virgil

❧

Love ya mega lots.

❧

Ti amo!
("I love you" in Italian.)

❧

To my tasty BLT
(Big Loving Teddy bear.)

❧

Yes indeedy, you're my sweetie.
Love, tweetie.

Tired of the same old same old? Find creative ways to say "I love you."

To my spice <u>guy</u>:
You're hotter than cayenne pepper.

∽⟨⟩

In the words of Uncle Sam,
I want YOU. (Bad.)

∽⟨⟩

The day I <u>cherish</u> you most?
Any day ending in "y."

∽⟨⟩

Who said it had to be the Fourth of July
to marvel at fireworks?

∽⟨⟩

You are <u>wonderful, smart</u> and <u>gorgeous</u>.
Guess you take after me.

Get 100 blank business cards. Write notes. Leave one around the house every day.

Romance & Fun

You're not the same person you used to be.
You're way better.

∽

If life's most treasured gift is love, you've
given me the best present in the world.

∽

I felt this magical moment
as we strolled the beach: My sandal
wasn't hurting my big toe anymore.

∽

You make my eyes roll back.
(That's a good thing.)

∽

I must admit, you're growing on me.
[Give with a plant.]

You don't have to be a poet to put your love in words.

Things you're good at:
Listening. Laughing. Loving.
(List to be continued...)

❧

You're great. I'm grateful to know you.

❧

A philosopher once said,
"We learn only from those we love."
Thanks for the lessons.

❧

I know it may sound sappy, but I want to
make you as happy as you've made me.

❧

There's this streetcar.
It's named desire. I'm on it.

Check the Encouragement section, page 63, for more ideas.

Romance & Fun

When you've got the greatest
<u>husband on earth</u>, it's easy
being the greatest <u>wife on earth</u>.

༄

One word describes how I like
being with you. Often.

༄

To boldly go where no <u>wife</u>
has gone before.

༄

The world is as it should be.
And I am a happy <u>man</u>.

༄

I think you're <u>funny</u>. You think
I'm <u>demented</u>. What a team.

See Fast Phrases, page 140, for quick words to show your love.

10.
Sympathy

The sense that somebody cares always
helps because it is the sense of love.
~ George E. Woodberry

Deeply sharing the grief of your loss.

Wishing I could be with you to hold
your hand and give you a hug.

When I heard about <u>the accident</u>, I cried
an ocean of tears. I will miss <u>Jennifer</u>.

Our sincere sympathy to everyone at
the <u>Riviera Company</u> on the loss of an
outstanding <u>leader</u> and <u>friend</u>.

To personalize a message, insert your own words where <u>underlines</u> appear.

I didn't have the pleasure of knowing
your <u>grandfather</u>. But from what you told <u>me,</u>
<u>I</u> know how much he was loved
and will be missed.

∽

Extending <u>our</u> sincerest condolences.

∽

How sad <u>I was</u> to learn of your <u>mother's</u> death.
If she was anything like you,
she was <u>quite a lady.</u>

∽

<u>Our</u> deepest sympathy to you <u>and your family</u>
at this painful time.

∽

Please know <u>I'm</u> thinking of you fondly.

If you were close to the deceased, share your positive memories in a note.

Raising <u>six</u> children is a tribute of love
reserved for a few special people,
including your <u>mother</u>.

∽

Losing your <u>father</u> so soon is a huge heartache.
You're close in our thoughts.

∽

In honor of an <u>uncle</u> whose sense of humor
will always <u>keep our hearts chuckling</u>.

∽

<u>I</u> can't find the words to express <u>my</u> sorrow
over the death of your <u>husband Gus</u>. He was a
<u>kind, caring man</u> and a <u>good neighbor</u>.

∽

A tearful goodbye to a loving <u>aunt</u>.

For related messages, see the Thinking of You section, page 125.

With <u>energy, enthusiasm and creativity</u>,
<u>John</u> made life <u>less stressful and more joyful</u>
for <u>lots of people</u>, especially <u>me</u>.

❦

Each life is touched by others. With some, the
touch is warm and loving and lingers forever.
That is how <u>Gloria</u> touched me.

❦

It was an honor knowing and working with <u>Jim</u>,
a true <u>Southern gentleman</u> if ever
there was one.

❦

<u>Monica</u> had an incredible talent for many
things. <u>I</u> will always remember the <u>smiles</u> she
brought to everyone around <u>her</u>.

❦

Knowing <u>Mrs. Jefferson</u> made <u>my</u> life <u>richer</u>.

You can't go wrong when you write from your heart.

Fondly remembering <u>Joyce</u>, a delightful lady
with <u>a joyful, soaring spirit</u>.

∾

May <u>her</u> incredible life be a reminder to us all
that one person CAN make a difference.

∾

<u>Malcolm</u> is our hero. He served our country
with integrity, honor and courage.

∾

<u>John</u> will be remembered for many things,
but mostly for the beautiful force
of <u>his</u> spirit and love.

∾

<u>Julie</u> was as good a mother as <u>God makes</u>.
<u>Her</u> life will forever cast a loving glow
on <u>Adam, Jenny and Elise</u>.

Your words can be a big comfort to those who are grieving.

} Sympathy

Many caring thoughts
are with you at this moment.

∾

<u>Our</u> faith, love and support
are here for you today and always.

∾

With sympathy, understanding and prayer.

∾

<u>I</u> pray that your treasured
memories of <u>Bill</u> will keep you strong.

∾

This is the time you need
your friends the most. I'll bring over dinner
<u>for you and the kids</u> on Thursday.

To stay in touch, send another note a couple weeks after the funeral service.

Holding you close in <u>our</u> prayers during
your time of sorrow.

☙

Extending our <u>deepest sympathies</u> and
prayerful assurances.

☙

God's peace to you.

☙

May <u>Jack's</u> spirit find as much joy in its
journey as <u>he</u> found in life.

☙

May you be comforted
in the light of love, today and
during the <u>tough road ahead</u>.

Be sincere. Let your words flow from your true feelings.

Remembering <u>Tarita</u> and all the ways
<u>her</u> life touched <u>ours</u>.

◦~◦

An enormous loss for <u>your family</u>.
And for <u>all of us</u>.

◦~◦

Your heart has been broken
in the most painful way.
<u>I'm</u> sorry.

◦~◦

Peace be with you at this time of loss.

◦~◦

Stay strong.
You're close in <u>our</u> thoughts.

For more sympathy ideas, see Fast Phrases, page 141.

11.
Thank You

Appreciation can make a day. Even change a life.
~ Margaret Cousins

<u>Kindness</u> comes from the heart.
It also comes from you.

Look up "<u>generous</u>" in <u>my</u> dictionary and you
will see something amazing: your name.

Your <u>thoughtfulness</u> took weeks
off my recovery time.

On a scale of <u>marvelous</u> to <u>fantastic</u>,
you get a triple <u>stupendous</u>.

To personalize a message, insert your own words where you <u>underlines</u> appear.

Thank You

I can't thank you enough. But I CAN keep
on loving you for the rest of my life.

&

Words could never express <u>my gratitude</u> to
you for being so <u>nice</u> to <u>Al and the kids</u>
while I was <u>in the hospital</u>.

&

Extra thanks for your extra <u>kindness</u>.

&

What the world needs now is
more <u>generous souls</u> like you.

&

Your many acts of caring
have restored <u>my</u> faith in the human race.

It always feels good to count your blessings. Why not count them in a note?

words to the rescue ⟩ Thank You

If my stomach could clap,
it would give you a standing ovation.

❧

I've got two words for people who can
grill a steak like you. A-Mazing.

❧

We have umpteen blessings to
be thankful for. You top the list.

❧

Earth to Becky: Your New Year's party
was out of this world.

❧

We could never repay you for the way you
made us feel welcome. But we can sure try.

For more Thank You ideas, see Fast Phrases, page 142.

Uncle Steve:
Thanks for the birthday money.
I love it. And you.

❧

You made us say WOW a million times.
Thanks for the show tickets.

❧

I honestly don't know many people as kind
and considerate as you. (Except maybe me.)

❧

Thanks for the treat.
My taste buds echo the sentiment.

❧

Twenty-one salutes. Three cheers.
And one big thanks.

Thank You notes are fun to get. Send them for little things as well as big.

Thanks for the shopping spree...
from the bottom of <u>my</u> cart.

∽

You are light years beyond any kind of
"<u>fantastic</u>" word <u>we</u> can think of.

∽

You've given me something
a dentist would charge big bucks for.
A gleaming smile.

∽

You may claim to be a mere mortal.
But to me, you're nothing less
than an angel.

∽

Your <u>gift</u> felt like <u>manna from heaven</u>.

Do you have an attitude of gratitude? Share it. Write a note.

Your generosity
makes my heart <u>sing opera</u>.

～○

You've made me so happy,
my cheeks hurt from smiling so much.

～○

<u>We saw God's grace</u> in all the <u>caring</u>
<u>people</u> like you that reached out to <u>us</u>.

～○

It was <u>an extraordinary effort</u>.
But no less than <u>we all</u> know
you're capable of.

～○

You just made <u>an old lady</u> want to
<u>do the hula hoop</u>.

See Fast Phrases, page 142, for more Thank You ideas.

words to the rescue ⟩ Thank You

Thank you from the bottom of
my beer mug.

⌒

Thank you for loving me just the way I am,
while challenging me to be all I can be.

⌒

Our appreciation to a coach who's
always on the ball.

⌒

You've been a lifesaver to me.
My hope is to return the flavor some day.
[Give with colored roll candy.]

⌒

Two small words. A great deal of gratitude.
Thank you.

Running behind? It's never too late to send a Thank You note.

Thank You

Thoughtful is as thoughtful does.

❧

I feel like a kite dancing in a blue sky.

❧

With a million thanks to my many friends,
and all those who supported, cheered and kept
me awake these last couple months.

❧

It's not a holiday or special occasion.
But you're a person worth praising.
Thanks for all you do.

❧

Oceans of thanks.
And a skyful of appreciation.

Don't have a greeting card? No paper? Cut one out of a paper shopping bag.

⎰ Thank You

Van Gogh said, "Great things are not done by impulse but by a series of small things brought together." Thanks for <u>leading the team</u>.

∽

Your oration is worthy of an ovation.
Please accept <u>our enthusiastic</u> appreciation.

∽

My biggest, grandest blessing? You and everyone else <u>who so selflessly volunteered</u>.

∽

You have a heart the size of a <u>football field</u>.

∽

I thought I was giving to you. But I ended up getting more than I could have imagined.

Thanking a friend? Find lots of ideas in the Friendship section, page 73.

When it comes to <u>people</u> with big hearts,
you can't be beat.

❧

People like you are born givers.
People like me are honored to help you
fulfill your destiny.

❧

It's an understatement to say
how overjoyed I am.

❧

I firmly believe the more you bless others,
the more you are blessed. Guess that makes
you a blessings millionaire.

❧

Shazam, you're good.

Be specific. Tell the giver exactly why you appreciate their gift.

Thank You

The only possible way <u>we</u> can pay you back
is to <u>just keep loving you</u>.

❧

<u>Y</u>our exceptional <u>organizational skills</u>
combined with your <u>unending enthusiasm</u>
helped make <u>this project</u> a <u>huge success</u>.

❧

A big ol' thanks.

❧

Thanks for adding so much to my life.
Like the extra <u>five pounds</u> from
your <u>irresistible</u> meals.

❧

The universe isn't big enough
to hold all the <u>gratitude I</u> feel.
<u>My</u> heartfelt thanks to <u>all</u>.

Give them a smile. Send a Thank You note when one isn't expected.

Thank You

Gluttony is so good.
Thanks for the <u>feast</u>.

∽◦

My favorite part of <u>the weekend</u>?
Everything.

∽◦

Holy hectic. You really know
how to get the job done.

∽◦

The thrill of victory. The agony of
two left feet. Thanks for the dance lesson.

∽◦

You just made <u>my</u> day...week...
month...and year.

For more Thank You ideas, see Fast Phrases, page 142.

12.
Thinking of You

Gentle words, quiet words, are
after all, the most powerful words.
~ George E. Woodberry

My heart has a mind of its own.
It won't stop thinking about you.

Hoping my <u>positive brain waves</u> meld with
yours to help you <u>get through this</u>.

In <u>my</u> thoughts, you're never more
than <u>a whisper away</u>.

My mind deserves a raise. It's working
overtime worrying about you.

To personalize a message, insert your own words where <u>underlines</u> appear.

Thinking of You

You occupy my thoughts 24/7.
So I'm building a permanent room
for you in my brain.

❧

Always know, <u>I</u> care.

❧

Thinking of you takes my pulse
off the charts.

❧

I wanted to send you a warm fuzzy.
But I couldn't find one at the store,
so this <u>note</u> will have to do.

❧

Thinking of you lovingly, longingly.

Don't have anything to write a note on? Be creative. Use a paper napkin.

Thinking of You

My thoughts are like a boomerang.
They always return to you.

∽

A great hue is the color blue.
But not so good when you're feeling it.

∽

A sunbeam to warm you, a moonbeam
to charm you, a sheltering angel
so nothing can harm you.
~ Irish blessing

∽

Happy Wednesday to my wife,
who makes every week easier to get through.

∽

Though my thoughts often wander, they
usually wind up at the same destination: You.

You don't need a special occasion to tell someone you care.

Thinking of You

Tons of people are rooting for you.
<u>I'm</u> at the head of the pack.

❧

I just heated up some nice warm
thoughts of you.

❧

From the top of my head to the tip
of my toes, all of me is thinking of you.

❧

A boatload of good thoughts are splashing
through the universe on their way to you.

❧

120% totally devoted 2U.

You can't go wrong when you write from your heart.

Thinking of You

You've been on my mind so much,
my brain hurts.

You may be a thousand miles away,
but in my thoughts I'm holding your hand.

If thoughts were <u>flowers</u>, you'd be floating
in a sea of <u>red roses</u>.

You're always on my mind...
and my screensaver.

<u>My</u> thoughts are focused on you <u>today</u>,
because nothing in this world
is more important.

See Fast Phrases, page 143, for more Thinking of You ideas.

To get the right word in the right
place is a rare achievement.
~ Mark Twain

Fast Phrases

When you need help pronto, flip to the
following pages. They're packed with
hundreds of phrases to get your pencil
in high gear. Browse all the sections so
you don't miss a thing.

Pleasant words are as an honeycomb,
sweet to the soul and health to the bones.
~ The Bible

fast phrases — Anniversary

Perfect pair
Couple of winners
Dynamic duo
50 years, 50 cheers
My marvelous mate
Growing old together
You, me, destined to be
My pillar, my pal
Our date to celebrate
Still insane about you
The one I adore
Stir crazy in love
We made it kiddo
Smitten with you
To my huggy hubby
A legacy of love
Together forever
Two hearts, one love
Beautiful dreamer
Kudos and congrats
Fun times, sad times

Faith, family and friends
Team Smith
Milestone in life
Keep the flame burning
Honorable achievement
Commemorate the date
Just plain good folks
A proud family
Blessings of a lifetime
Hats off to mom and dad
Your kids salute you
We honor your union
Together like glue
Match made in heaven
Our total admiration
An example to follow
Genuine commitment
A bond blessed by God
Good going you two
My warmest wishes

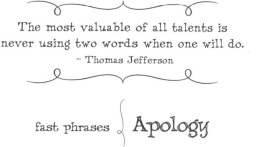

The most valuable of all talents is
never using two words when one will do.
~ Thomas Jefferson

fast phrases ⎰ Apology

Me airhead. You right.	Regret my actions
I come to you humbly	Honest remorse
I was a royal jerk	Totally my fault
What was I thinking?	Pardon my blunder
You were 100% right	Please excuse my...
I deeply regret...	I ask your forgiveness
Excuse my pea brain	Let's bury the hatchet
Sincere apology	How sorry I am
Call me butthead	I take full responsibility
Sooooooo sorry	Let me make it up to you
Off my rocker	Ooopsie daisy
Out of my mind	An honest mistake
I eat my words	Unavoidable accident
Get my act together	Unfortunate error
Control my temper	Long story short, I goofed
Acted like a fool	I plead for your pardon
Poor judgement	Changing my ways
All I can say is duh	I realize now...
One more chance	An inexcusable error
I'm heartbroken	Slipped my memory
I slipped up	I admit it's my fault

A kind word is like a spring day.
~ Russian proverb

fast phrases 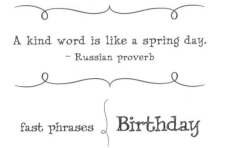 **Birthday**

Warmest regards	Not a kid anymore
Cheers to the old guy	You look mah-velous
Three letters: F-U-N	More lovely each year
What's your secret?	Indulge, it's your day
Happy milestone	You age darn well
Totally teen	Bravo, birthday boy
Terribly 20	How many candles?
22? Good 4U	A hug and a wish
High-five 25	It's the BIG one
Flirty 30	Age is just a number
Yipeee 33	Whoop it up
Fab-You-lous 40	Livin' the good life
Nifty 50	Rx for happiness
Sexy 60	To an ageless soul
Scintillating 70	Age...it's all relative bro
Crazy 80	Handsome at any age
Nothing like 90	You old geezer
A relic I relish	Warmest blessings
There's still hope	40 is the new 20
Spry for your age	You're better than ever
No "fine wine" jokes	Someday, when you're old...

Kind words are worth much and they cost little.
~ Author unknown

fast phrases

Congratulations

Way 2 go	Hail to the victor
Couldn't be more proud	She shoots, she scores
Absolutely awesome	Lifetime of happiness
Sharing your joy	Mr. Achievement
Continued success	Ms. I-can-do-anything
Sincere accolades	You amazing. Me #1 fan.
Darn right I'm proud	Praises all around
Good news. Good 4-U.	You earned it every step
Applause applause	We're in awe of you
You richly deserve it	Mr. Capable
A rare achievement	Mr. Never-say-never
Compliments to all	Enjoy the ride
Another slam dunk	A lifetime of dreams
Enjoy the spotlight	Follow your bliss
Warm wishes	You wear success well
A huge step forward	You never stop amazing
Life changing moment	The joy of winning
Hey diva	Extra pat on the back
Top of the heap	Feather in your cap
Top dog	Best of the best
Talent always pays	Deepest admiration

> Words of encouragement fan the spark of
> genius into the flame of achievement.
> ~ Wilfred A. Peterson

fast phrases **Encouragement**

You're the best
Keep on keepin' on
Because you're you
Stand tall. Stand proud.
The sun in Sunday
Persistence pays
Here to support you
Lean on me
Earned your wings
Rooting for you
Hang in there
We're cheering you on
Woo woo woo
Keep being you
Be strong and confident
Keep the faith
Grow from mistakes
Live and learn
A fresh new start
Get up and get going
Get your mojo back

Back in the saddle
Seize the dream
You're in the groove
Stay focused
You're a fighter
Remember your roots
Nobody does it like you
Brush yourself off
Go get 'em tiger
Knock their socks off
Show 'em your stuff
Your star is shining
This is your moment
You're almost there
You've come so far
Top of your game
You're in the zone
Stretch to the limit
You've got the power
Support from above
New and improved you

Brevity is the soul of wit.
~ Shakespeare

fast phrases { **Friendship**

Oh pal of mine	Perfect partners
From your #1 fan	Peas in a pod
My homeboy/homegirl	Tragically hip
Buds 4 life	Two of a kind
You guys rock	Blessing of friendship
Co-horts in silliness	Rare connection
Laughing all the way	Joined at the hip
Yep, we're tight	The mod squad
Odd couple	Together we're better
Crazy compadre	Sharing life and laughs
Cool. Friend. You.	Nutty buddies
True and genuine	The trouble tribe
You the man	The vibe is right
You go girl	Friends for all seasons
Partner in crime	A meaningful bond
Three kindred spirits	Pals since childhood
Five reasons I like you...	The four Musketeers
Awesome amigo	Drinking buddies
One heck of a man	Guys from the hood
Meaning of friendship	You're my kind of people

There's a great power in words, if you
don't hitch too many of them together.
~ Josh Billings

fast phrases } Get Well

Take care, friend.
Bear hugs 2 U
Rest up. Recover fast.
Healing wishes from all
Thoughts and hugs
Thank your doctors
Take your medicine
You're greatly missed
Praying for the best
Sorry you're down
Mend well, friend
Glad the worst is over
I want to see you well
You'll bounce back
Bandages of love
Back to full strength
Tougher than nails
One day at a time
Pamper yourself
Out of commission
Back to your old self

Warm blankets
The rainbow is coming
Laughing = Healing
Watch funny movies
The warmth of the sun
Good for body and soul
Meditate on beauty
Prescription for health
God's healing hand
Re-invigorate your body
Soothing music
Keep yourself hydrated
Stress-free wishes
The miracle of healing
Feel your strength
Indulge in rest
My on-the-mend friend
Worried about you
Embrace the healing
Enjoy the downtime
Hey smiley face

Good things, when short, are twice as good.
~ Baltasar Gracian

fast phrases **Goodbye & Miss You**

Toodles	Happy for your new job
Godspeed	A hearty kum-by-ya
Farewell friend	Happy days
Safe travels	Be good to yourself
What'll we do without you?	Remember the fun we had
Lotsa luck, lotsa love	Embrace the opportunity
So sad to see you go	Follow your heart
Don't forget me	Miss you mega lots
Bye bye birdie	All messed up missing you
Adios	Miss you missy
Au revoir	Get back here ASAP
Bon voyage	Welcome back anytime
Ciao	Dizzy missing you
Cheerio	Missing you bad
Sayonara	Mostly I'm blue
I wish you adieu	Counting the days
Have an excellent life	Yearning to see you
Stay as sweet as U R	Craving your return
Two hearts apart = tears	Surviving day by day
Soul 2 soul	Accchhh! I'm losing it.
More than you know	Lonely and sad

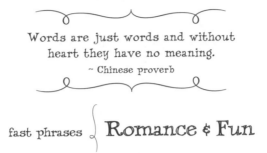

Words are just words and without
heart they have no meaning.
~ Chinese proverb

fast phrases ## Romance & Fun

You're 100% huggable	Best a guy could have
You rock my existence	Souls in alignment
Love ya big time	Shelter in your arms
Sunlight for the soul	Enriched by you
Not a lovey dovey guy	My wonder-filled wife
Tiger, you're grrrrrreat	To my bald eagle
This crazy connection	My wild untamed lion
My partner in crime	My bearded wonder
You elevate my life	Beautiful baby face
A fun soul to be with	My wild dreamer
The admiration is mutual	Heavenly hubby
Created to be crazy	I love the one I'm with
Love ya long time	You illuminate me
Your wacky ways	This weekend?
Joys of being us	Five things I like about...
My heart sings	Two crazy people in love
Our affection connection	My forever protector
Loving you, just because...	Exclusively yours
Well melt my heart	This thing we have
Always and forever	Two-gether we're better
With a smile...	Tonight?

A fated sorrow may be lighted with words.
~ Latin proverb

fast phrases Sympathy

Deepest condolences
Sincere sympathy
So sad and so sorry
Thoughts are with you
Close in our thoughts
A hug across the miles
You have our support
Thinking of you fondly
With sorrow for your loss
Know that we care
Our heartfelt prayers
Supporting you always
Caring, gentle thoughts
Grieving with you
Hugs of support
With friendship
A profound loss
God's peace be with you
Remembering fondly
We're so sorry about...
We're crying with you

The hurt you must feel
Losing someone so close
My heart is so very sad
An honor to know
I'll never forget
We've lost a great one
A life I admire
A hole in our hearts
Loved her deeply
My heart aches
An exemplary person
Wish I could be there
Celebrating the life of
In memory and love
Cherished memories
Strength from above
In loving tribute
So hard to lose a father
The comfort of friends
Senseless tragedy
Unbearable pain

Words are the voice of the heart.
~ Confucius

fast phrases { Thank You

A big ol' thanks
I'm 110% impressed
More than you know
Gracious x 100
My true gratitude
You made us smile
So kind of you to...
Heartfelt appreciation
More than I could ask
Your presence is a present
This boy is overjoyed
Your support lifted me up
How did you know?
An angel on earth
Humongous hugs 4U
We're on cloud 10
Bravo to my benefactors
Your gift hit the target
My soul says thanks
You generous. Me thrilled.
Insanely thoughtful

Exactly what I needed
It's about gratitude, dude
Standing Ovation x 10
Bless you for your kindness
Thank God for you
Cue the applause
You hit a homer once again
Thoughtfulness = You
Kindness is contagious
We'll never forget it
Your goodness glows
Gifted at gift giving
We salute your kind heart
Tons of appreciation
A zillion and one thanks
Our hearts are brimming
I tip my hat to you
Holy cow, you're cool
My heart overflows
Man, that was nice

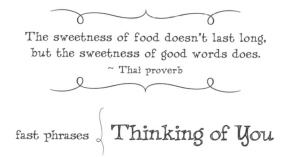

The sweetness of food doesn't last long,
but the sweetness of good words does.
~ Thai proverb

fast phrases Thinking of You

Hugs and thoughts
Wishing you serenity
Rest assured, I'm here
Thinking of you 24/7
How-deeee
Someone who cares
Comfort and peace, friend
Wish you were back
Concerned and worried
My heart is with you
Thoughts and hugs
Warmest wishes
Happy brain waves
Remembering the magic
You're always with me
Constantly in my prayers
Heart, mind and soul
Concentrating on you

I not only care, I care
Happy Friday eve
Happy Saturday
Pondering our tomorrow
Relishing the future with you
Happy day before tomorrow
I'm under your spell
Hope you're well
Missing you in a big way
What matters in life? You.
Your #1 admirer
I carry you in my thoughts
Every day, I pray for you
Saluting your awesomeness
Bouquets of best wishes
Always part of my heart
The fire's still burning
Popping in to say hi

Thank you

If it takes a village to create a book, I have a tribe to thank. To Kathy Hyink, ACSW, for your unending encouragement and insights into human nature, which helped shape the tone and scope of this book. To Kathleen Ferres and Cheryl Poole for your friendship and continuous contributions starting over fifteen years ago. To David Barlow and Ilya Hardey for your support and design expertise, without which I could not have finished this project. To the best editor/proofreader in the world, Peter Artemas. To Carol Graham for your amazing understanding of people and language. To my sisters Janine Dailey, Mary Fadie and Anne Marie DeFrain, and brother Gordon Fadie, who reviewed umpteen book covers and kept me going with wit and wisdom. To my friend, the indefatigable Susan White for guidance during early versions of this book and years of "watercooler advice."

To Rene DuFord, AIFD, who first encouraged my entrepreneurial trek in Grand Rapids, Michigan. To my favorite cheerleaders: Mark, Linda, Cathy, Dolores, and Ann Moynahan; Kathy Sheldon and Carol Caron. To my ad agency comrades, especially Kim Brauer, Ken Cendrowski, Greg Clancey, Victoria Croumie, Laura Kosciuszko, Donna McGuire, Kim Steffan, MaryAnne Simmerer and Kristin Wicks: You amaze me with your talent and helpfulness. To friends, family and associates, too many to name, who contributed or inspired verses, or filled out surveys, my sincere gratitude. For the best service a new publisher could hope for, kudos to Dave Friesen at Hignell Press. Finally, thanks to my parents, Gordon and Phyllis Fadie, for the freedom to follow my own path.

Did you write or receive a great note?

Tell us about it. We're looking for creative, touching, witty, sentimental, humorous and silly short notes for the next edition of *Words to the Rescue.*

It may be a card you received with flowers, a message scrawled on a greeting card, or a note from your spouse you found in your briefcase.

Notes must be original and be 50 words or less. Please do not send quotes. If your note is used in a future edition, you will receive a complimentary copy. All submissions become the property of Orange Sky Books.

E-mail your submissions to:
steve@WordsToTheRescue.com

About the author

Steve Fadie is passionate about the power of words. A former senior writer at one of the nation's leading ad agencies and lifetime Michigan resident, he is a fan of HGTV, Native American proverbs, and mint chocolate chip ice cream. He holds a degree in communications from Michigan State University.

Dear Reader:

Since this is a book about notes, I could not end these pages without writing you one. My thanks for picking up *Words to the Rescue*. Over the last 15 years I've had tons of fun working on it. (Hey, good things take time.) If you have suggestions for future editions or just want to say "hi," I'd be honored to hear from you.

Write me at steve@WordsToTheRescue.com

Enjoy.

Steve Fadie

Do you know anyone who could use a few good words?

- Words for personal notes
- Words for Facebook pages
- Words for email and e-cards
- Words for office greeting cards
- Words for handmade cards
- Words for birthday cakes
- Words for toasts
- Words for shout-outs
- Words for lunch box notes
- Words for scrapbook pages
- Words for gift inscriptions
- Words for floral enclosure cards

Give a gift they'll use all year.

To purchase copies of *Words to the Rescue*

and *Words to the Rescue 2*, visit

www.WordsToTheRescue.com

Free! "Words of the Week" email from Steve Fadie

To receive timely words of inspiration throughout the year, sign up now for Steve's Words of the Week.

www.WordsToTheRescue.com

Use these pages to collect favorite words and quotes, to remind yourself of important dates, and to record which messages you sent to whom, so you don't repeat.

Notes:

Notes

Notes

Notes

Notes

Notes

Notes

Notes

Notes

Notes

Kind words can be short and easy to speak
but their echoes are truly endless.
~ Mother Teresa